POC
PUB W

Hampshire

Nigel Vile

COUNTRYSIDE BOOKS
NEWBURY BERKSHIRE

First published 2006
© Nigel Vile, 2006

COUNTRYSIDE BOOKS
3 Catherine Road
Newbury, Berkshire

To view our complete range of books,
please visit us at
www.countrysidebooks.co.uk

ISBN 1 85306 958 2
EAN 978185306 958 1

Designed by Peter Davies, Nautilus Design
Produced through MRM Associates Ltd, Reading
Printed by Information Press Ltd, Oxford

Contents

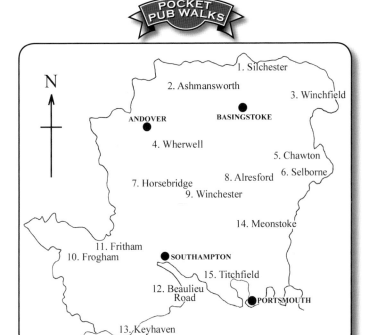

POCKET PUB WALKS

N

1. Silchester
2. Ashmansworth
3. Winchfield
ANDOVER
BASINGSTOKE
4. Wherwell
5. Chawton
6. Selborne
8. Alresford
7. Horsebridge
9. Winchester
14. Meonstoke
11. Fritham
10. Frogham
SOUTHAMPTON
15. Titchfield
12. Beaulieu Road
PORTSMOUTH
13. Keyhaven

Area map showing location of the walks

Introduction

What better way to spend a leisurely few hours than to stretch your legs and then visit a traditional pub for a delicious meal or snack and a glass of beer or wine? The fifteen circular walks in this book allow you to do just that. Each route takes you through some of the finest scenery in Hampshire, and then guides you to a watering hole, recommended for its food and hospitality.

In the north of the county, we have rolling chalk downland, with extensive views and open vistas. To the east, on the Surrey and Sussex borders, the beech hangers are typical of the local landscape. There are, of course, the noted river valleys, carrying chalk streams that are much sought after for their fly-fishing. The Test and Itchen, the Avon and the Meon, are all prized rivers with crystal clear waters. There is the coast, too, with its desolate and remote salt marshes and secretive inlets. And last, but not least, is the open heathland and oak woodland that makes up the New Forest, arguably the most-loved corner of the county.

It is not just the natural landscape that will catch the eye, however. There are the delightful villages, with timber-framed and thatched cottages and historic churches. There are elegant Georgian market towns, ancient ports and cities, cathedrals and abbeys, hill forts and restored canals.

The walks are between 3 and 7 miles in length. Car parking has been suggested in the vicinity of each pub, although in many cases it will be possible to use the pub car park. Do please remember, though, to seek the landlord's permission first – in case parking is at a premium – and promise to return for a meal and a drink.

To make your day complete, don't forget to carry a snack and a drink in that trustworthy rucksack, as well as a decent set of waterproofs. Despite occasional belief to the contrary, the authors of walking guidebooks cannot guarantee their readers sunny weather! And remember that rain creates muddy paths. No publican wants a trail of mud through the lounge or public bar so do attempt some form of wash and brush-up, if necessary, before entering these fine hostelries.

It just remains for me to wish you many happy hours of pleasure following these pub walks.

POSTSCRIPT

I can be contacted through my website. If you have problems with any of these walks, please email me and any necessary amendments will be posted up in order to help other readers and users of this book. The website address is www.geocities. com/vilewalks/nigel

Nigel Vile

Publisher's Note

We hope that you obtain considerable enjoyment from this book; great care has been taken in its preparation. Although at the time of publication all routes followed public rights of way or permitted paths, diversion orders can be made and permissions withdrawn.

We cannot, of course, be held responsible for such diversion orders and any inaccuracies in the text which result from these or any other changes to the routes nor for any damage which might result from walkers trespassing on private property. Sadly also, changes of landlord and pub closures are not uncommon. We are anxious, though, that all details covering the walks are kept up to date and would therefore welcome information from readers which would be relevant to future editions.

The simple sketch maps that accompany the walks in this book are based on notes made by the author whilst checking out the routes on the ground. However, for the benefit of a proper map, we do recommend that you purchase the relevant Ordnance Survey sheet covering your walk.

1 **Silchester**

The Calleva Arms

Calleva – **the site of a Roman town** on the fringes of Silchester – comes as a real surprise. Walking across country from Silchester Common and Pamber Wood, these vast chalk and flint walls that enclose a site of some 100 acres suddenly come into view. Although none of the Roman buildings survive to this day, excavations have revealed the true extent of this most historic of sites. On the edge of the Roman town, outside the stone walls, is a rural amphitheatre built around AD 50-75 and able to seat about 3,000 people. A delightful little museum – passed along the way – contains a collection of displays that interpret what is one of the finest Roman sites in Britain. Silchester Common and Pamber Wood are delightful locations too. Deep, lonely woodland, secretive streams and an abundance of wildlife combine to form what is a much-loved nature reserve.

Hampshire

Distance – 6 miles.

OS Explorer 159 Reading, Wokingham and Pangbourne. GR 628621.

Woodland tracks, lanes and fieldpaths that cross an undulating landscape.

Starting point The Calleva Arms.

How to get there 8 miles east of Newbury, follow the A340 south for 2 miles to Aldermaston, before following signposted unclassified roads to Silchester. Park in the centre of the village in the car park by the village hall, opposite the Calleva Arms pub.

THE PUB

The Calleva Arms in Silchester is part of the George Gale Hampshire Brewery estate. An idyllic pub facing the village green, the former name of the Crown was changed in recent years to commemorate the historic Roman site of Calleva that features on this walk. As well as traditional pub fare, a visit to the Calleva Arms will enable you to sample such excellent Gale brews as the Horndean Special Bitter and Butser. Butser Hill is the dominant hill of the local downs, through which the pure brewing water has been filtered before being pumped to the well in the heart of the Horndean Brewery. The Calleva Arms can also boast an award-winning family garden.

Open 11 am to 3 pm and 5.30 pm to 11 pm Monday to Friday. Open all day Saturday and Sunday.
☎ *01189 700305*

1 Follow **Pamber Road** past the **Calleva Arms** before taking the first left – **Dukes Ride** – just past the pub. In 150 yards, where the road bears slightly left into an estate, keep ahead along a footpath to a gate at the entrance to **Silchester Common**. Follow the main woodland path ahead for 600 yards until it drops down to cross a stream on a wooden causeway. Continue ahead on the main woodland path for 150 yards to a crosstrack, cross the stile opposite and enter Pamber Forest. Keep ahead to a footbridge and, having crossed a stream, keep ahead for 75 yards to a junction. Follow the right-hand of the two paths opposite, and continue for 600 yards to a major crosstrack,

The Roman amphitheatre seated about 3,000 people.

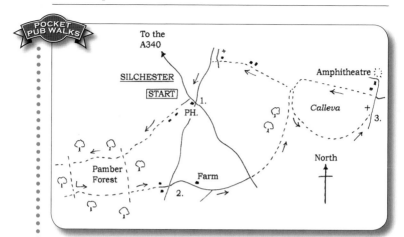

ignoring a minor path crossing the track 100 yards before. Turn left, and follow the track ahead for 350 yards to a major crosstrack, before turning left and continuing along another track for 600 yards to a gate by Silchester Sewage Treatment Works, ignoring all side tracks along the way. Follow the lane ahead for 400 yards to a crossroads.

2 Follow the lane opposite towards **Silchester Farm**, to reach a junction in ¾ mile, ignoring one right turn along the way. Cross the stile in the hedgerow opposite, follow the right edge of the field ahead to its corner and a pair of stiles. In the next field, cross to the far-left corner by **Dickers Copse**, enter the adjoining field and head directly across to a handgate and stile at the entrance to a belt of trees. Walk through the trees to a handgate, before crossing the next field to a handgate opposite. Continue through another belt of trees before heading up the right edge of the next field to a handgate in the top corner. Turn right to reach the enclosure that was the site of the Roman town of Calleva. Pass through a handgate on the right, and follow the course of the Roman walls anti-clockwise for ½ mile to a gate and stile and a lane.

3 Follow the lane ahead to **Silchester church**, and keep ahead to a left-hand bend in 200 yards. On the bend, pass through a handgate on the right to explore the Roman amphitheatre. Retrace your steps back towards the church and, in 100 yards, just before a lane on the left, turn right along a gravel track. Follow this track to a series of gates, pass through the left-hand gate and follow the gravel path as it winds its way around a barn on the left. Continue along this track as it crosses the site of the Roman town – surrounded by the town walls – to reach a junction on the far side of the enclosure. Keep left – and shortly right – to a handgate, and continue along the track away from Calleva. Follow this track for 600 yards to a junction by the **Calleva Museum**. Cross the road and follow a track opposite through scrubland to reach another road. Turn left back to Silchester Common and the car park.

Places of interest nearby

On the Hampshire/Berkshire border near Silchester lies the elegant Stratfield Saye House, home to the Dukes of Wellington since 1817. View the fascinating collection of paintings and furniture and see the wonderful Wellington Exhibition featuring his magnificent funeral carriage and displays charting his military and political life.
☎ *01256 882882 for details of opening times.*

The Vyne, a National Trust property south of Silchester, was built in the 16th century for Lord Sandys, Henry VIII's Lord Chamberlain, and then became home to the Chute family for over 300 years. Through the artistic and aesthetic interests of its various owners, it has been at the cutting edge of the development of country house architecture, interior design and taste.
☎ *01256 883858 for details of opening times.*

2 Ashmansworth

The Plough Inn

The **North Hampshire Downs** are often referred to as the 'Hampshire Highlands'. There is obviously a slight use of poetic licence here, but this is certainly an area of fine hillwalking. Ancient tracks cross chalk downland that rises to well over 900 feet above sea level, with fine outlooks and vistas at every turn. Ashmansworth, the highest village in Hampshire at over 750 ft above sea level, stands on the fringes of this upland area. Attractive brick and thatch properties line the long main street that runs through the village, with St James church lying just off the walk to the south of the village green. The composer Gerald Finzi (1901-1956) lived in the property opposite St James, and is buried beside the porch. There is an engraved glass window in the porch by Laurence Whistler dedicated to English

Distance – 7 miles.

OS Explorer 144 Basingstoke, Alton and Whitchurch. GR 415575.

Quiet lanes, tracks and fieldpaths crossing the North Hampshire Downs.

Starting point The Plough Inn.

How to get there Ashmansworth lies west of the A343 between Newbury and Andover. Follow the signposted unclassified roads into the centre of the village, and park on the roadside in the vicinity of the Plough Inn.

music. The surrounding landscape truly inspired Finzi, whose music often reflects the beauty of this corner of England.

THE PUB

The Plough Inn is quite simply a no-frills pub that regularly receives plaudits from CAMRA. Two quarry-tiled rooms have been knocked into one, with patrons able to drink fine real ales tapped from the cask and eat simple home-cooked food. Archers Best Bitter and Golden are on offer, together with a guest beer.

With its log fire and absence of piped music, the Plough is one of a dying breed of traditional English pubs. There has been regular talk of its closure and conversion to a residence, but to date these plans have been thwarted. As the old adage goes 'Use it or lose it'.

Open 12 noon to 2.30 pm (not Tuesday) and 6 pm to 11 pm.
Sunday 12 to 3 pm and 7.30 pm to 10.30 pm.
Closed Monday.
☎ *01635 253047*

Hampshire

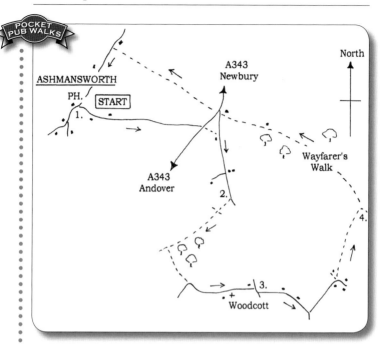

North

A343
Newbury

ASHMANSWORTH

PH.

START

1.

A343
Andover

2.

Wayfarer's
Walk

4.

3.

Woodcott

1 Follow the road opposite the Plough signposted to Andover, a side lane off the main road in the village. After ¾ mile, cross the A343 and follow a footpath opposite that goes up a bank alongside a fence. At the top of the climb, bear left into an open field and follow the edge of this field to its far-left corner, before continuing on an enclosed path alongside a property down to a lane. Turn right, and follow this lane for just over ½ mile to a bridleway on the right, 300 yards past the cul-de-sac on the right leading to Crux Easton.

2 Follow this bridleway, initially it is an enclosed track that, in 120 yards, enters a field. Continue down the right edge of this field to a crossing of paths in the corner. Follow the track opposite that runs along the left edge of a field. In the far left corner of the field, immediately past the end of **Beech Hanger Copse**, turn left to follow a signposted path that runs alongside the western edge of the woodland. In the bottom corner of the field, having passed a green hut on the right, continue ahead along an enclosed track down to a gate and quiet lane. Follow the lane uphill for 500

The Hampshire Downs afford some fine hill-walking.

yards to reach **St James church** in Upper Woodcott. Continue along the lane for 150 yards to a junction.

3 Turn right and, almost immediately, left along the lane to Woodcott and Dunley. In ¼ mile, keep left at a fork just past some pylons, and drop down towards **Lower Woodcott**. At the bottom of the hill, where the lane bears right into the village, turn left along a track. In just a few yards, turn right to follow a bridleway on the right up out of the valley. Follow this track for ½ mile to a point where it bears sharply to the right. At this point, pass through a gate on the left and follow the **Wayfarer's Walk** across the left-hand edge of a hillside field. On the far side of the field, just past a belt of trees on the left, join a track that comes uphill from the valley bottom on the right.

4 Continue ahead along this track for almost 1½ miles to a lane by **Keeper's Cottage**. Follow this lane to the right for a few yards down to the A343. Turn left, and almost straightaway right, to continue following the Wayfarer's Walk. Having reached a lane in ¾ mile, turn left and head back into Ashmansworth, reaching the Plough Inn after ½ mile.

Places of interest nearby

Highclere Castle, one of England's most beautiful Victorian castles, lies just a mile or two north-east of Ashmansworth. It stands on the site of an earlier house that, in turn, was built on the foundations of the medieval palace of the bishops of Winchester who owned this estate from the 8th century. Highclere was purchased in 1679 by Sir Robert Sawyer. He bequeathed it to his daughter in 1692. Her marriage to the 8th Earl of Pembroke brought Highclere to the Herbert family, ancestors of the Earls of Carnarvon.
For more details ☎ *01635 253210.*

3 **Winchfield**

The Barley Mow

The Basingstoke Canal is generally regarded as one of the most beautiful in the United Kingdom. In the January 1997 edition of *Waterways World* it was stated that the Basingstoke Canal provides 'the perfect antidote to modern living', the opportunity to 'relax among the lilies, the kingfishers and endless dragonflies' and to enjoy a 'level of peace and tranquillity which is becoming harder to find'. This walk explores an all-too-short section of this fine waterway, that was built to connect the Hampshire market town of Basingstoke with the River Thames via the River Wey Navigation. Away from the canal, the walk passes through Dogmersfield Park, where our steps border a fine expanse of water known as Tundry Pond. The estate's manor house, now a hotel, is renowned for being

Distance – 6 miles.

OS Explorer 144 Basingstoke, Alton and Whitchurch. GR 778538.

An easy walk along canal towpaths and level fieldpaths.

Starting point The canalside car park opposite the Barley Mow at Winchfield.

How to get there *Leave the A287 two miles east of Odiham and follow a road northwards to Dogmersfield. At a junction in the village, keep left towards Winchfield. In ¾ mile, turn left into a cul-de-sac opposite the Barley Mow pub. Immediately on the left is a car park by the Basingstoke Canal.*

Hampshire's finest meeting venue. As you step out across the estate, you will readily appreciate why such praise has been heaped upon this handsome landed estate.

THE PUB **The Barley Mow**, a fine white-painted Georgian hostelry, has a most traditional feel and atmosphere. In addition to the dark beams and carved brick hearth, photographs of local sports teams adorn the inn's walls. The bar menu might typically include baguettes and pâtés, curries and fish dishes, while the evening meals are more in keeping with restaurant food. There is always a range of real ales available, including Courage Best and Young's Special, Old Speckled Hen and Abbot Ale.

Open 11 am to 2.30 pm and 6 pm to 11 pm. Food is served from 12 noon to 2 pm and 7 pm to 9 pm.
☎ *01252 617490*

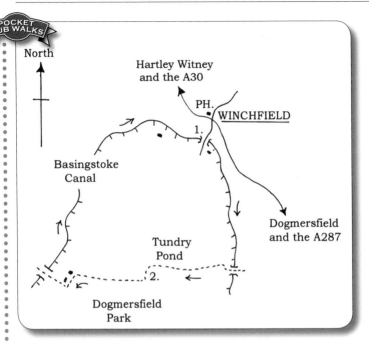

POCKET
PUB WALKS

North

Hartley Witney
and the A30

PH.
WINCHFIELD

1.

Basingstoke
Canal

Tundry
Pond

Dogmersfield
and the A287

2.

Dogmersfield
Park

1 Walk up to the canal, turn left and follow the towpath for 1¼ miles to a brick bridge. Leave the towpath, cross the canal by means of this bridge and walk ahead to a gate. Beyond the gate, follow an enclosed path to the right down to **Tundry Pond**. Follow the path alongside the southern edge of this lake for 350 yards to a handgate at the far end of the lake. Away to the left is a former manor house – now the Four Seasons Hotel – that dominates **Dogmersfield Park** in which this lake lies.

2 Beyond this handgate, follow a gravel road away from the lake for 100 yards to a junction of tracks. Take the gravel track on the immediate right, and follow its enclosed course towards **Sprat's Hatch Farm**. In 150 yards, veer slightly right off the gravel road to follow an enclosed footpath to a handgate and lane by the

Hampshire

farmhouse. Turn left, and follow a private road – public bridleway – that soon bears right. In 250 yards, the track reaches a bridge over the canal. Cross the bridge, turn right and follow the towpath ahead for 1 mile to **Barley Mow Bridge**, passing under two other bridges along the way. The car park is on the left just past this bridge.

Places of interest nearby

Basing House was once the country's largest private house, the palace of William Paulet, 1st Marquess of Winchester, who was Lord Treasurer of England under three Tudor monarchs. The Civil War brought disaster to Basing which fell to Oliver Cromwell in 1645. The ruins contain Norman earthworks, the remains of Tudor kitchens, cellars, towers, a 300-foot long tunnel, a spectacular barn, Civil War defences designed by Inigo Jones and a recently re-created 16/17th-century formal garden.
☎ *01256 467294 for further details.*

The Willis Museum in Basingstoke. Travel back in time, and experience some of the major changes that have created the Basingstoke that we know today. Contrast the present with the past, the rich with the poor.
☎ *01256 465902 for details.*

Peace and tranquility on Tundry pond.

4 **Wherwell**

The White Lion Inn

Located in the Test Valley, Wherwell is a most delightful place. With its thatched cottages overlooking the village green and its war memorial, a fine old inn and a priory on the site of a nunnery founded by Queen Elfrida in the 10th century, there is much of interest in the village itself. Bordering the Test on the fringes of Wherwell is Chilbolton Common, a picturesque water meadow on the upper reaches of the river. Rich in flora and fauna, these meadows have never been subject to agricultural 'improvement'and are a reminder of the traditional meadowland habitat. In the neighbouring valley lies the River Anton, a chalk stream whose waters remain ever-popular with trout fishermen. With open hilltops and expansive views, paths that border sparkling

Distance – 5½ miles.

OS Explorer 131 Romsey, Andover and Test Valley. GR 389409.

Lanes, riverside paths and fieldpaths that cross the undulating landscapes of the Test and Anton Valleys.

Starting point The White Lion in Fullerton Road in Wherwell.

How to get there Leave the A303 as it bypasses Andover and follow the A3057 south towards Stockbridge. After 1 mile, turn onto the B3420 for Wherwell. Drop down into the village and immediately after the White Lion Inn, turn right into Fullerton Road and park on the roadside in the vicinity of the pub.

rivers and a section of the 'Spratt and Winkle Railway Line' – a victim of the Beeching cuts that ran from Andover to Southampton – this is a walk with interest and surprise at every turn.

The White Lion Inn, with its beamed bar and open fire, Delft plates and brassware, is all one would expect of a traditional village inn. The bar food ranges from soup and ploughman's through to fish, steak and chicken dishes, whilst the range of real ales might typically include Adnams Best or a local brew such as Ringwood Best. For those warm summer days, the White Lion has courtyard and terrace seats, perfect suntraps to enjoy a rest and refreshment following a stroll in the Test valley.

Open 12 noon to 2.30 pm (3 pm on Saturday) and 6 pm to 11 pm (7 pm to 10.30 pm Sunday).
☎ *01264 860317*

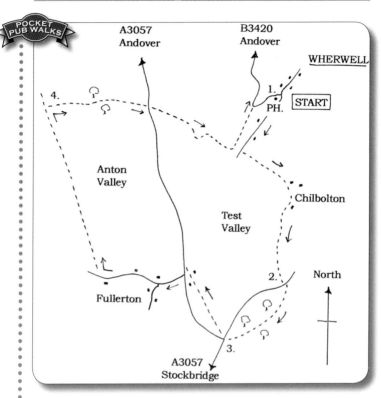

1 Continue along Fullerton Road away from the pub for 500 yards to a left turn, a bridleway signposted the Test Way. Turn left, cross a footbridge over the River Test and enter **Chilbolton Cow Common**. Walk ahead across the common, following a well-defined path, to reach a bridge over a tributary stream of the Test in 400 yards. Cross this bridge, and follow the path to a parking area. Follow the unmetalled road out of the parking area to reach a junction, turn right and follow another unmetalled road along to a whitewashed cottage. Walk around the right of the cottage and up to a playing field. Turn right immediately before the playing field entrance to

follow an enclosed path for 150 yards to a handgate. Enter the playing field, turn right to a gate in the end boundary and continue along an enclosed path for 400 yards to a seat on a small green.

2 Turn left along the road for a few yards then right into **West Down Countryside Park**. In just a few paces, turn right through a gap in the fence and follow a path up a grassy slope towards some woodland on the hilltop. On the hilltop, bear half left to take the furthest left of several paths into the trees. In 25 yards, at a wooden barrier, keep ahead to reach a red marker post in a small clearing. Walk across to another red post on the far side of the clearing and, ignoring a concrete road going off to the left, follow the path ahead back into the woodland. On reaching the next red post, follow the right edge of the clearing ahead to another red marker post in the far corner. At this point, follow the path downhill to the right to reach a wooden barrier and a parking area.

3 Turn right onto a road, cross to a brick wall opposite and follow a Test Way sign downhill to an old railway line. Follow the trackbed to the right – the Test on the left – for 450 yards to reach a driveway that gives access to some properties. Follow this driveway ahead to reach the **A3057**. Turn left, follow the main road with care until, just past an old railway bridge, turn right towards Longstock. In 150 yards, keep right at the next junction towards Redrice and continue along a quiet lane for 350 yards to reach **Fullerton Manor** on the left. At this point, follow a track into a field on the right and continue on the track along the left edge of two fields for 600 yards to reach a wooden barrier, all the while walking along the hillside above the **River Anton**. Beyond the barrier, follow the field boundary ahead downhill to reach a track at the bottom of the field. Follow the track to the left for 200 yards to a point where a path goes off to the right.

4 Turn right through a handgate, and walk to a footbridge over a river. Continue following the path as it bears right to reach another footbridge, this one crossing the **River Anton**. Cross the

Hampshire

Bridge over the River Test.

river, and walk through a belt of trees to reach the corner of a field. Turn right, and follow the right edge of the field to a gate in its corner, and the A3057. Cross the road to a path and handgate opposite, and walk uphill in the field ahead to a handgate in the top right corner. Continue along a path which soon bears right along the edge of the hilltop. This path shortly bears left and right before continuing its enclosed course across the hilltop to emerge into a field. Follow the path as it bears left to follow the end of the field downhill. Keep on this uncultivated strip as it bears right to reach a track and old railway bridge at the end of the field. Do not pass under this bridge – instead keep left and follow the bridleway along the bottom edge of the field to reach a gap in the far-left corner. Follow the right-hand boundary of the next field for 350 yards, passing gardens on the right, until the path leaves the field to follow a track down to the **B3420**. Turn right, and follow the road down into Wherwell, turning right past the White Lion to return to your vehicle.

Places of interest nearby

The Hawk Conservancy at Weyhill near Andover is one of the premier bird of prey parks in the United Kingdom. It is well known for the flying displays which take place each day during the open season. There are three flying displays each day at 12 noon, 2 pm and 3.30 pm.
☎ *01264 772252*

5 **Chawton**

The Greyfriar

In a letter to her sister Cassandra, Jane Austen wrote 'and the plan is that we should all walk with her [Harriet Benn] to drink tea at Farringdon'. Whilst we may not be taking tea at Farringdon, this delightful walk enables us to follow in the footsteps of Jane Austen and to explore the countryside that so influenced and shaped her novels. Chawton was where Jane Austen spent the last eight years of her life from 1809 until 1817, living with her mother and sister, as well as their great friend Martha Lloyd. Her third brother – Edward – inherited the landed estate at Chawton, and the walk across country to Farringdon passes both the mansion and its grounds. In Farringdon, All Saints church was where the naturalist Gilbert White – a great friend of the Austens – was curate from 1761 until 1784. There were frequent walks between the two villages as the families spent many hours together. Altogether a fascinating literary excursion in a delightful corner of Hampshire.

THE PUB

The Greyfriar sits opposite Jane Austen's house in Chawton and is, as would be imagined, an archetypal 'old wooden beam' type of hostelry. It is, to quote the publicity material, 'the type of place where time seems to have stopped and you can while away the hours over a great pint and some astonishing home-cooked food'. The lunch menu features typical bar meals, whilst in the evening a most imaginative restaurant style menu appears. Being a Fuller's inn, a pint of the flagship London Pride ale is almost obligatory.

Website: www.thegreyfriar.co.uk
Open 12 noon to 11 pm (10.30pm Sunday).
☎ *01420 83841*

Distance – 4 miles.

OS Explorer 133 Haslemere and Petersfield. GR 709376.

A gently undulating landscape, with no steep hills.

Starting point The public car park alongside the Greyfriar at Chawton.

How to get there Leave the A31 at a roundabout just south of Alton – a junction with the A32 – and follow the turning into Chawton village. The public car park is clearly marked.

1 Leave the car park and turn left along the cul-de-sac signposted to St Nicholas church and **Chawton House**. On reaching the driveway on the left leading to the church, the road ahead is blocked by a barrier. Continue along this road – it is a public right of way – for 200 yards until the road approaches the

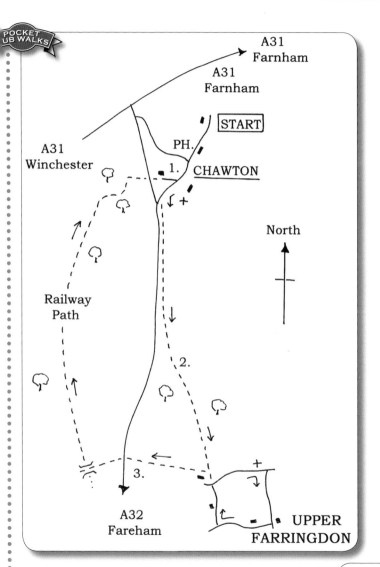

POCKET
UB WALKS

A31
Farnham

A31
Farnham

START

A31
Winchester

PH.

1. CHAWTON

+

North

Railway
Path

2.

3.

A32
Fareham

+

UPPER
FARRINGDON

busy A32. Where the road ends, continue along a footpath on the left to reach a stile on the left, and a permissive path bordering the main road. Follow this permissive path for 350 yards to the next stile and enter an open field. Turn left, and head uphill to a stile in the top field boundary at the entrance to **Noar Copse**.

2 Follow a track through Noar Copse, continue across an arable field and on into **Berryhill Plantation**. Beyond this woodland, continue on the track as it drops down into Upper Farringdon. On reaching a crossing of tracks by some properties, follow the path ahead down to its junction with a road – Parsonage Close. Turn left to a junction with Church Road, turn left again and walk through the village, passing a folly on the right and the church on the left. At the next junction, turn right into Crows Lane and walk down to a junction by the Rose and Crown inn. Turn right along The Street, and continue to its junction with Church Road. Head down to the junction with Parsonage Close, turn left to a telephone box and then right back up to the crossroads passed earlier on entering the village. Turn left, and follow a track across country for 600 yards to the **A32**.

3 Follow the lane opposite that runs alongside **Farringdon Cottage**. In 300 yards, just before an old railway bridge, follow a stepped path on the right down to the old trackbed. Follow the trackbed in a northerly direction for just under 1 mile. Where the enclosed trackbed ends, keep ahead along an uncultivated strip of land that runs across an arable field. In 150 yards, bear right and continue along the path to reach a small beech copse. Bear left through this copse to a stile, turn right and follow the right edge of a field down to a stile and the A32. Cross the main road to a stile opposite, and follow the right edge of the field ahead down to a stile in the corner. Follow a short section of path alongside a property down to **Ferney Close**, and continue down to a junction. Turn left back into the centre of Chawton.

Places of interest nearby

The Curtis Museum in Alton first opened to the public in 1865 and is the second oldest in Hampshire. It moved to its present location in 1880, and houses an enthralling local collection acquired by Dr William Curtis (1803-1881) and his associates in the local Mechanics' Institute. The displays include prehistoric tools, Roman pottery reconstructions, Saxon burials, the Battle of Alton 1643, the notorious tale of Sweet Fanny Adams, and hop picking and brewing.
☎ *01420 82802 for details.*

Watercress Line. The Mid-Hants Railway runs steam trains from Alton to Arlesford, with Thomas the Tank Engine special days. The line is an excellent attraction for anyone wanting a dose of nostalgia!
☎ *01962 734866 for details or visit the railway's website on www.watercressline.co.uk.*

Jane Austen's House is a pleasant 17th-century house in the pretty village of Chawton not far from her birthplace of Steventon. The museum houses an attractive collection of items connected with Jane and her family including the table that she used when writing her novels. There is some of her jewellery, and examples of her needlework skill. In the drawing room is a fine Hepplewhite bureau-bookcase and chairs that belonged to Jane's father and came from the rectory at Steventon. The bookcase contains some first editions of Jane's novels.
☎ *01420 83262 for information or visit www.jane-austens-house-museum.org.uk*

Chawton House.

The Queens Inn

I t was **Gilbert White**, that well-known naturalist, who placed Selborne very firmly on the map. Born in Selborne at his grandfather's vicarage, White spent much of his life studying and writing about the local natural history. His best-known work – *The Natural History and Antiquities of Selborne* – has merit both as a natural history handbook and a work of literature. His home – now a museum – sits opposite St Mary's church, in whose grounds lie not only White's grave but also the stump of a yew tree which, when it was destroyed in the gales of 1990, was

Distance – 3½ miles.

OS Explorer 133 Haslemere and Petersfield. GR 742344.

One steep climb onto Selborne Hanger, followed by a walk through a quiet valley.

Starting point The signposted public car park just off the B3006 in Selborne. The Queens Inn lies on the main road, a very short walk from the car park.

How to get there Selborne lies on the B3006, 4 miles south of Alton. There is a signposted public car park at the southern end of the village.

1400 years old and over 26 feet in girth. Away from the village, the walk explores the landscape that was so much loved by Gilbert White. Steep hillsides and ancient woodland, with beech and oak trees, lie above the diminutive Oakhanger Stream. It is a landscape that has changed little since White's death in 1793.

THE PUB **The Queens Inn** at Selborne, a traditional Ushers hostelry, is sure to catch the eye of the passing motorist with its bright whitewashed exterior. With its fine garden, comprehensive facilities and renowned restaurant, few visitors to the Queens will come away disappointed. The menu extends from lighter snacks such as whitebait or brie wedges through to substantial offerings such as lemon sole and mixed grill, whilst the lounge and public bars will always have at least four real ales on offer.

Website www.queens-selborne.co.uk
The Queens is open all day, with food served until 9.30 pm.
☎ *01420 511454*

1 Walk down to the car park entrance, and take a sharp right turn along a path signposted to the **Zigzag and Hanger**. Follow this path up to a gate at the entrance to Selborne Common and, beyond this gate, turn left and follow the steep zigzag path to the top of the hill. Turn right along a slightly stepped path running through the trees to a fork in 25 yards. Keep to the right-hand path into a beech wood. Keep on the woodland path for 600 yards until it drops down to a junction, a National Trust

The landscape at Selborne has changed little since Gilbert White's day.

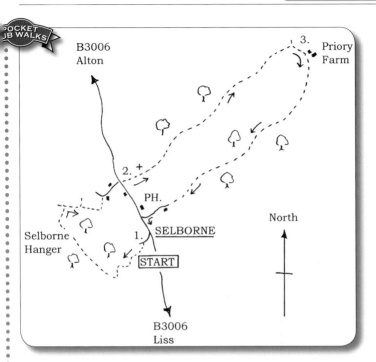

sign on the left. Turn right and, in 200 yards, where the track bears left, turn right to a stile. Enter a field, turn left and follow the left edges of three fields to a stile and enclosed path. Follow this path – it shortly bears left – down to a lane. Turn right along to the **B3006**.

2 Cross the main road, and follow the footpath signposted Hangers Way into the churchyard. Cross to a gate in the far right corner of the churchyard, before following a path down to a bridge over **Oakhanger Stream**. Continue along a woodland path to a gate, cross a small field to a gate opposite and enter the Long Lighe. Follow the path ahead that borders woodland on the left and meadow on the right for 500 yards to a gate and open field.

Hampshire

Head to the far right corner of this meadow, pass between two lakes to a stile, and continue along a path that bears right into **Combe Wood**. Continue along this woodland path to a stile, before following the left edge of the next field to a stile and track.

3 Turn right down to **Priory Farm**, and keep on the track that runs to the right of – and then away from – the farm buildings. In 30 yards, where the lane bears left, keep ahead along a track to a gate. Continue along a grassy path that runs along the left edges of two fields before reaching a handgate and woodland. In ½ mile, cross a gate and continue along the lane to the B3006. Turn left to the car park, or right to reach the Queens Inn.

Places of interest nearby

The Curtis Museum in Alton first opened to the public in 1865 and is the second oldest in Hampshire. It moved to its present location in 1880, and houses an enthralling local collection acquired by Dr William Curtis (1803-1881) and his associates in the local Mechanics' Institute. The displays include prehistoric tools, Roman pottery reconstructions, Saxon burials, and hop picking and brewing.
☎ *01420 82802 for details.*

Gilbert White's House and the Oates Museum are located in the centre of Selborne. A charming 18th-century country house, home of famous naturalist Revd Gilbert White, author of *The Natural History and Antiquities of Selborne*, the beautiful garden has been recreated to 18th-century form. Elsewhere in the house, the Oates Museum commemorates Captain Lawrence Oates, who went with Scott to the Antarctic and also Captain Oates' Victorian Uncle Frank, who journeyed to South America and South Africa.
☎ *01420 511275 for further information.*

7 Horsebridge

The John of Gaunt Inn

Horsebridge lies deep in the Test Valley, a mile or two south of Stockbridge. A noted chalk stream, the Test is widely regarded as the birthplace of modern fly fishing, with Halford, Plunkett Greene and Skues immortalising the river in their writings. Across the fields from Horsebridge lies the delightfully-named village of King's Somborne, and with such a title this settlement is certain to have regal origins. The manor was a royal property for centuries, and as it was recorded in the Domesday Book as Somborne Regis, it was probably a royal possession in Saxon times. John of Gaunt's Deer Park lay between the River Test and King's Somborne and, in the field alongside the church, the humps and bumps represent the site of John of Gaunt's palace. A gentle climb over the hills to the west of the village brings our walk to the former Andover to Romsey railway line, known affectionately as the 'Spratt and Winkle', so-named because seafood was transported along this route from the south coast. Now part of the Test Way, the path borders the River Test back into Horsebridge, a relaxing end to a fine walk.

Hampshire

Distance – 4 miles.

OS Explorer 131 Romsey, Andover and Test Valley. GR 345305.

Fieldpaths, lanes and a railway path in the Test Valley.

Starting point Test Valley Way car park at Horsebridge.

How to get there Follow the A3057 south from Stockbridge for 3 miles to King's Somborne. Continue south from the village for another ½ mile before turning right along the lane signposted to Horsebridge. In ½ mile, turn right in the village down to the John of Gaunt Inn. Turn left in front of the inn along an unmetalled road that leads to a Test Way car park.

THE PUB **The John of Gaunt Inn** is a delightful whitewashed cottage-style property, with an L-shaped bar and traditional features that include a welcoming log fire in winter months. The John of Gaunt offers good attractively-priced food – such as shepherd's pie and steak and kidney pudding – whilst the selection of real ales might include Palmers or Ringwood Best Bitters. One critic commented that it was 'the sort of pub you could imagine in a fifties B movie', a fine description for a simple and unpretentious pub that has a timeless and unspoiled feel.

Open Monday to Friday 11 am to 3 pm and 6 pm to 11 pm.
Weekends open all day.
No food Sunday evening or Monday.
☎ *01794 388394*

King's Somborne has regal origins.

1 Walk to the John of Gaunt, and turn right up to the main road to **King's Somborne**. Turn left and, immediately past the first pair of cottages, cross a stile on the left. Follow the right edge of the field ahead to a gate in its far right corner. Continue along an enclosed path at the rear of some properties to the next handgate, before following an enclosed path along to a bungalow on the left and a handgate. Cross the next field to a wooden barrier opposite, before following an enclosed path running behind another group of properties to reach an open field. Walk the length of this field to a gate and the A3057.

2 Cross the main road to an enclosed footpath opposite that runs between properties. Follow this path for 150 yards through to a road, ignoring one right turn. Turn right and, in 50 yards,

Hampshire

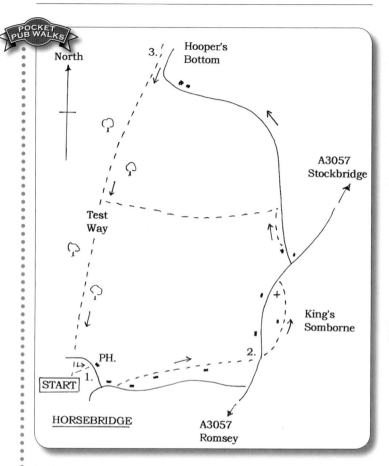

before a property called **Greenacres**, turn left along a grassy track. At the end of this track, pass through a wooden barrier on the left into a park. Walk across to a handgate just beyond the children's play area, before heading across the next field to a stile and the village church. The humps and bumps in this field mark the site of **John of Gaunt's palace**. Walk around to the front of the church and rejoin the A3057. Follow the main road to the right for 150 yards before turning left into Cow Drove Hill. Just after the last house on the left, climb some steps on the left up a bank into a field. Turn right, and follow the right edge of this field uphill to a road junction in 300 yards. Ignore the left turn to How Park Farm – instead, follow the main lane ahead across the hill and down to **Hooper's Farm**. Continue along the lane past the farm for 350 yards to a barrier on the left-hand side.

3 Turn left and join the **Test Way** – it follows the course of an old railway. Follow the Test Way to the left for 650 yards to a barrier and continue ahead along an unmetalled road. In 250 yards, where this road bears left, pass through a gateway ahead and follow the former trackbed ahead for ¾ mile to a road in **Horsebridge**. Cross this road, and follow the Test Way for 100 yards to a junction by the former Horsebridge Station. Turn left along an unmetalled lane back to the Test Way car park.

Places of interest nearby

Just north of Horsebridge is the Houghton Lodge Gardens and the Hampshire Hydroponicum. Set in an idyllic spot on a hillside above the River Test, visitors will find a fully restored walled kitchen garden, a topiary peacock garden and a topiary dragon which puffs at you as you pass. There are herbaceous borders, woodland and river walks, a hydroponic greenhouse, and an orchid display house. Hydroponics is a form of gardening in which plants are grown without the use of soil. Instead plants are successfully grown in a nutrient enriched perlite and vermiculite base.
☎ *01264 810912 for details of opening times.*

The Bell

Alresford – literally the ford over the river where the alder
trees grow – is a delightful market town located on the
River Alre. Pronounced 'Allsford', this beautiful Georgian
town enjoyed prosperity based upon the wool trade for many
years. Old Alresford is mentioned in the Domesday Book, but the
present town of New Alresford did not come into existence before
1200 at the time when the Great Weir was being built to create Old
Alresford Pond as a reservoir for the Itchen Navigation. The colour-
washed Georgian houses that line Broad Street and West Street,

arose from the ashes of a series of great fires in the 17th century. To the north of the town lies rolling open countryside, and it is here – along the River Alre and its feeder streams – that we find vast watercress beds. Watercress-growing became industrialised in the 1860s following the undercutting of cereal crops by imports of cheap maize, and the simultaneous arrival of the railway to carry the perishable cress to distant destinations. The local line – known as the Watercress Line – enabled the cress crops to be transported to markets in London and beyond. Following the closure of the railway in 1973, a group of enthusiasts rallied around to preserve the line, which today operates nostalgic steam traction between Alresford and Alton.

THE PUB

The Bell, a freehouse dating from 1767, was originally a Georgian coaching inn. Fronting onto Alresford's West Street, its handsome exterior – with fine floral displays – readily catches the eye of the passing traveller. The atmosphere at the Bell is relaxed and informal, and centres on the provision of fresh seasonal produce cooked to order. With its extended bar and dining room, well-kept beers and friendly service, the Bell is

Distance – 5½ miles.

OS Explorer 132 Winchester. GR 588325.

Gentle walking across an undulating landscape.

Starting point The public car park alongside Alresford Station (fee payable).

How to get there Leave the A31 six miles east of Winchester, drive into the centre of New Alresford and follow the signs for the Watercress Line. This will take you via Station Road to Alresford Station, where there is a pay-and-display car park.

quite the perfect place to relax following a gentle stroll through the watercress country of Hampshire.

Website www.bellalresford.com
The Bell is an hotel as well as a free house, and as a consequence is open all day. Food is served between 12 noon and 2 pm and 7 pm and 9.30 pm.
☎ *01962 732429*

1 Walk down Station Road to West Street, turn right and take the first left into Broad Street. Towards the bottom of Broad Street, veer left into a cul-de-sac called Mill Hill. In 50 yards, turn left

Cows take it easy on the watermeadow near Alresford.

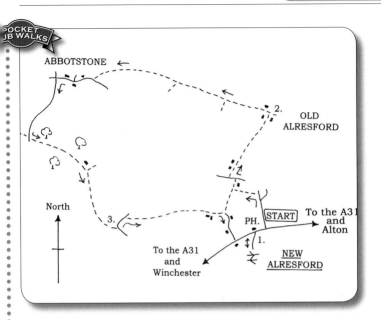

into Ladywell Lane. Follow this lane – it becomes a gravelled path - for 300 yards along to a thatched property spanning the River Alre called **Fulling Mill**. Immediately past this property, turn right, cross the river and follow a gravel drive up to a quiet lane. Turn left along this lane and, in 100 yards, turn right onto a gravel track – a footpath – leading to a number of properties. Just before the last property, follow the left edge of a grassy area along to a stile, before following the right edges of the next two fields, cress beds behind the hedgerows on the right. Cross a stile in the corner of the second field, and continue along a track for 200 yards to a junction in front of a whitewashed cottage.

2 Turn left along **Ox Stone Drove**, and follow this track for 1¼ miles to a lane on the fringes of Abbotstone, ignoring two left turns along the way. Follow the lane ahead for 300 yards to a junction in the hamlet of **Abbotstone**, just past a brick-and-

Hampshire

thatch cottage. Turn left along the lane signposted to Itchen Stoke and Winchester. Follow this quiet lane for 600 yards and, at the top of a hill, turn left along a track – the Wayfarer's Walk. Follow this track for ¾ mile to a junction just past a cottage and a series of cress beds. Turn right, and follow what is still the Wayfarer's Walk for ½ mile to a lane.

3 Turn left and, in 40 yards, veer right off the lane to follow a footpath across a field bordering a belt of trees. Towards the far side of the field, keep right into the trees and continue along the path until it emerges onto a lane by some properties. Continue along the path alongside these houses, before dropping downhill to reach the banks of the **Alre**. Follow the riverside path for 400 yards through to a footbridge, before turning right into The Dean. Follow this road up to West Street, turn left and then first right into Station Road, opposite the Bell Inn.

Places of interest nearby

The Watercress Line, running from Alresford to Alton, offers a nostalgic trip back to the days of steam. Known more properly as the Mid-Hants Railway, at Alresford visitors will find a goods shed and shop, as well as a buffet and reconstructed goods office.

Full details of this heritage steam railway can be found on www. watercressline.co.uk or by telephoning ☎ 01962 733810.

The National Trust's Hinton Ampner Garden lies just south of Alresford. The personal vision of Ralph Dutton, 8th and last Lord Sherborne, innovative colour schemes and scented plants can be enjoyed alongside glorious vistas. The grand house contains a fine collection of Regency furniture and Italian paintings.

☎ 01962 771305 for details of opening times.

9 **Winchester**

The Wykeham Arms

This is a walk steeped in history. Not only is there the opportunity to explore Winchester, the ancient capital of Wessex and England, there is also the chance to visit the Hospital of St Cross. Founded in 1132, this, the oldest charitable institution in the country, includes a magnificent Norman church as well as the Brethrens' Hall and a medieval kitchen. To the south of Winchester – where the college and cathedral, St Alfred's statue and the guildhall will catch the eye – the walk explores a peaceful series of water meadows, bounded by the River Itchen and the Itchen Navigation. Overlooking this magnificent setting is St Catherine's Hill, with its Iron Age fort and 17th-century turf-cut maze. It is the view from this beautiful corner of Hampshire that will linger in the memory.

Distance – 4 miles.

OS Explorer 132 Winchester. GR 483280.

Gentle and easy walking, apart from a steep climb onto St Catherine's Hill at the outset.

Starting point The Tun Bridge car park below St Catherine's Hill.

How to get there *Just to the west of junction 10 on the M3 east of Winchester, there is a roundabout where the B3330 joins the A31. If you are coming from the south this roundabout can only be reached from the M3. At the roundabout, take the unclassified road heading west towards St Cross. In 500 yards, just before Tun Bridge and the Itchen Navigation, turn left into a car park.*

THE PUB

The Wykeham Arms, a many-roomed, Georgian hostelry alongside Winchester College and the Cathedral Close, is a treasure trove of antiquities – 2000 tankards, school canes, old school desks, mortar boards, cricket caps and more. Without a frozen ingredient in sight, the meals – such as smoked duck or roast rack of lamb – quite rightly earn rave reviews. A range of Gales Beers, the Hampshire brewery based in Horndean, are the natural choice for many customers. Trollope called the Wykeham Arms a 'third-rate hostelry', a remark that could not be further from the truth. How times have changed!

Open 11 am to 11 pm and 12 noon to 10.30 pm on Sunday.
☎ *01962 853834*

1 Walk to the end of the car park – away from the road – and turn left under an old railway bridge to reach the foot of **St Catherine's Hill**. Follow the track all of the way to the top, where the path emerges onto open ground, a turf-cut maze and beech copse in front of you. Follow the path to the right of the beech copse – fine views of water meadows to the right – until you reach the southern end of St Catherine's Hill. Follow a stepped path down the hillside to a gravelled track, and take this track down to the banks of the **Itchen Navigation**. Turn left, and follow the path that initially runs alongside this disused waterway. In 350 yards, turn left under an old railway bridge and continue along the track for 200 yards to a junction just before the M3. Turn right, and follow an old road signposted to St Cross. Follow this road to a footpath on the right, 150 yards beyond the river Itchen.

2 Turn right, and follow this path – initially a track leading to Mill House Farm and St Cross. In 80 yards, take the track on the right down to an old mill, bear left behind the mill buildings and join the banks of the river Itchen. Follow the riverside path for 250 yards to a stile, and join the footpath that runs alongside **St Cross**. Continue on this gravel path for ¼ mile until it reaches a road – handgates along the way – turn right to cross the river, and turn immediately left to continue following the river upstream. Keep on the riverside path for 600 yards until you reach the buildings of Winchester College. Turn right along the road running past these buildings and, at the next junction, turn left into **College Walk**. At the end of College Walk, turn left into College Street, passing more of the college buildings as well as the last residence of Jane Austen. At the end of College Street, with the Wykeham Arms on the left, turn right to pass through King's Gate, then immediately right through another archway leading into the grounds of **Winchester cathedral**. Follow the access road ahead that bears left all the while to reach the western front of the cathedral.

3 Having passed the impressive frontage of this historical building, continue along the path that leads down to Market Street and the Old Market Inn. Continue along Market Street to the **High Street**, turn right and follow the whole length of the High Street to reach the Guildhall and King Alfred's statue. Beyond a roundabout by the statue, continue along the High Street until you reach a bridge that crosses the Itchen. Immediately before this bridge, turn right to follow the **Riverside Walk** downstream until you reach Wharf Mill. Turn left on reaching the mill, cross the river and follow the road ahead to a junction. Turn right into Wharf Hill and, on a bend in 100 yards, follow the drive ahead that runs past Wharf House. In 50 yards, turn right along a footpath that drops down to the banks of the Itchen Navigation. Having crossed this waterway, follow the path to the left that borders the Navigation for ½ mile until you reach **Tun Bridge**. Join the road, turn left and cross the Itchen Navigation before turning right back into the car park.

St Cross Hospital, Winchester.

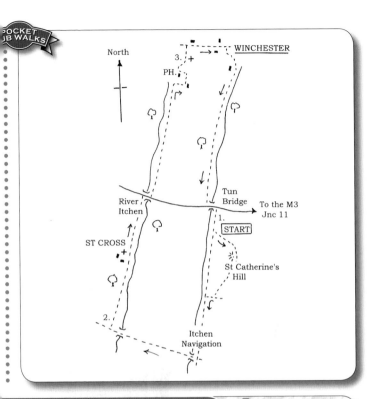

Places of interest nearby

There is so much to see and do in Winchester! As well as the magnificent cathedral and the City Museum, there are no fewer than five military museums in the area.

For details on all of these attractions – as well as St Cross Hospital – contact the Tourist Information Centre on ☎ 01962 840500 or go to www.visitwinchester.co.uk

10 **Frogham**

The Foresters Arms

The north-western corner of the New Forest is characterised by a series of parallel valleys separated by relatively high ridges. This excursion – surprisingly hilly for the New Forest – explores Latchmore Bottom, before climbing onto Hampton Ridge with its fine views across the open heathland. The valley bottom is a marvellously secluded place, watered by Latchmore Brook, where the Forest 'lawns' and running stream attract large numbers of New Forest ponies. Look out for 'Abbots Well' at the start of the walk, possibly a watering hole in centuries past for some wandering cleric on his way to or from Christchurch Priory. With its fine view of Hampton Ridge, the well is certainly an uplifting and inspiring place.

Distance – 3 miles.

OS Outdoor Leisure 22 New Forest. GR 177128.

Tracks and paths that cross the New Forest heathland and lawns. One climb onto Hampton Ridge.

Starting point A public car park 400 yards east of the Foresters Arms on the edge of the open forest.

How to get there *Just east of Fordingbridge, leave the B3078 Cadnam road and follow the unclassified lane signposted to Stuckton and Frogham. In Frogham, having passed the Foresters Arms, continue along the lane – now signposted to Abbots Well – for ¼ mile to a car park on the right-hand side of the road.*

THE PUB

The Foresters Arms in Frogham has been described by one critic as 'a real pub with real food and real ale'. This is an apt description for this ever-popular hostelry – part of the Wadworth estate – where customers are advised to look elsewhere if they require 'fast food'. With its flagstones and wood burning stove, comfortable dining room and pleasant garden, the Foresters is everything one would expect of an English hostelry. The menu ranges from sandwiches right through to a very popular Sunday lunch, with the range of beers including Wadworth's noted 6X.

Open 11 am to 3 pm and 6 pm to 11 pm.
☎ *01425 652294*

1 Leave the car park and turn right down the lane to **Abbots Well**. At the junction beyond the well, follow the track on the right signposted as a private road. In 350 yards, a drive on the right leads into a private residence. Continue ahead along the track

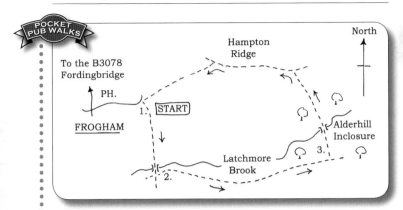

– passing a barrier – down to a footbridge across Latchmore Brook. Cross this stream and walk ahead into a car park called **Ogdens**.

2 Turn left through the car park and enter the open heathland. Walk ahead – there are few obvious paths in the forest – following a wide grassy expanse running parallel to **Latchmore Brook** on the left-hand side in the bushes. In just over 1 mile, an area of coniferous woodland called **Alderhill Inclosure** comes into view ahead. Follow the southern boundary of this woodland for 75 yards to reach a wooden handgate on the left at the entrance to the wood.

3 Follow the path ahead beyond this handgate – fording Latchmore Brook at one point – to reach another handgate at the northern end of the woodland. Follow the track ahead that climbs – bearing left all the while – to reach a junction on the hilltop in 550 yards. Turn left and follow this track across **Hampton Ridge** to a major junction of paths in ½ mile. Keep following the main track ahead as it bears left and then right downhill before heading across open heath to reach Abbots Well in ½ mile. Follow the lane ahead back to the car park.

Places of interest nearby

Fordingbridge Museum opened in August 2000 and is based on the Shering collection which was donated to the town in 1998. The Shering family built up the collection over many years and displayed it in a building in Shering's Yard. Displays of pictures and exhibitions of shops, brickyards and collections of objects from the old town feature prominently.

The Forest 'lawns' and Latchmore Brook.

☎ *Telephone 01425 655222 for more information.*

Breamore Manor House is located just north of Fordingbridge. The House was completed in 1583 by the Dodington family. It was subsequently purchased in the early 18th century by Sir Edward Hulse, a physician at the Court of Queen Anne, King George I and George II. The House has been lived in for the past 250 years by his descendants and remains very much the family home of the Hulses.

For information on the house and its Countryside Museum, ☎ *telephone 01725 512468 or visit the website at www. breamorehouse.com*

Rockbourne Roman Villa is located near Fordingbridge. It once stood in the centre of a large farming estate, and is the largest known Roman villa in the area. Its history spans the period from the Iron Age through to the 5th century AD.

Open from April to September, further information on the villa can be obtained by telephoning ☎ *01725 518541.*

11 **Fritham**

The Royal Oak

This **delightful walk** in the north-west corner of the New Forest encapsulates all that is best about the area – a forest village with its traditional pub, a fine pond with its feeder stream, deciduous woodland, open heath and a rich variety of wildlife. Eyeworth Pond is a beautiful stretch of water, enjoying a perfect location amid New Forest woodland. As well as attracting numerous wildfowl, the pond acts as a magnet for the forest's animals. It is a marvellous spectacle to see the local ponies wading into Eyeworth Pond, half-submerged in water, enjoying a cool bathe on a hot summer's day. The pond, incidentally, owes its existence to

Distance – 3 miles.

OS Outdoor Leisure 22 New Forest. GR 232141.

Tracks and paths that cross a level section of the New Forest.

Starting point The Royal Oak at Fritham.

How to get there 7 miles east of Fordingbridge and 3 miles west of Cadnam on the B3078, an unclassified road is signposted to Fritham. Follow this road across the open heathland for 1½ miles, following the signs for Fritham, to reach the Royal Oak. Park on the roadside in the vicinity of the inn.

the Schultze Gunpowder Factory which once had operations in the area. The company dammed the stream that runs through Howen Bottom to provide a water supply for their operations.

THE PUB **The Royal Oak**, with its whitewash and thatch, is one of the smallest and most intimate of hostelries in Hampshire. Steps lead up and down to small bar areas, where tables and stools, brickwork and inglenook fireplaces lend a real air of history and tradition to this ever-popular inn, the recipient of many CAMRA awards. Real ale is served from the wood, whilst the menu each day is displayed on a blackboard above the bar. The staple offerings are ploughman's, soups and pies, with food only normally available at lunchtimes. Despite its off-the-beaten-track location, the popularity of the Royal Oak is such that finding a table is often quite difficult!

Open 11.30.am to 2.30 pm and 6 pm to 11 pm (11am to 11pm on Saturday and 12 noon to 10.30pm Sunday).
☎ *02380 812606*

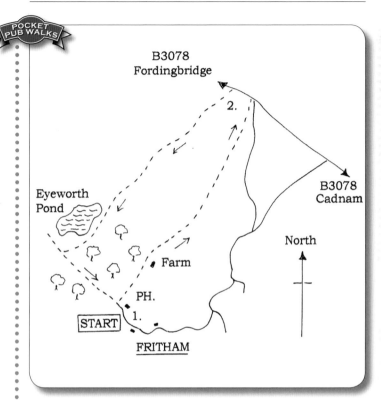

POCKET PUB WALKS

B3078
Fordingbridge

2.

Eyeworth
Pond

B3078
Cadnam

North

Farm

PH.

START   1.

FRITHAM

1 Walk northwards from the Royal Oak and, having passed the inn's garden on the right, turn right along a track signposted as giving access to a farm. Follow this track – it borders woodland on the left called **Howen Bushes** – for ½ mile until the track peters out and you emerge onto open heathland. Ahead there are no obvious paths – as is the case on much of the New Forest. Simply keep walking ahead across the open heath for ¾ mile to a point where a minor road coming from Fritham joins the B3078. The grid reference for this junction is **244156**.

2) Turn left, and follow the verge alongside the main road for 100 yards to a wooden barrier and gravel track going off to the left. Follow this track for 1¼ miles until it reaches a parking area alongside **Eyeworth Pond**. Follow the track alongside the pond to reach a quiet lane. Follow this lane to the left uphill for 600 yards back to the Royal Oak inn.

Eyeworth Pond enjoys a perfect spot in the New Forest.

Hampshire

Furzey Gardens and Will Selwood Gallery lie at Minstead, a few miles south of Fritham. The gardens comprise eight acres of delightful informal landscape with extensive views over the New Forest towards the Isle of Wight. There are beautiful banks of azaleas and rhododendrons, heathers, ferns, a water garden, the strange bottle brush tree, flaming Chilean fire trees and many other features including three delightful children's log cabins.

The Gallery is an interesting building of timber and thatch opened in 1974 to enable many local artists and craftsmen to display their work. There is an adjacent nursery run by the Minstead Training Project for people with learning disabilities and many of the plants and shrubs grown here are available for sale.

Visit the website on www.furzey-gardens.org for more information or telephone ☎ 02380 812464.

12 **Beaulieu Road**

The Beaulieu Road Inn

Beaulieu Road is little more than a halt on the Southampton to Bournemouth railway that serves the nearby Beaulieu Road Hotel. All around is nothing but heath and wooded forest. Five times each year, however, Beaulieu Road takes on a carnival atmosphere as dealers gather for the New Forest pony sales. This short walk explores the area to the south-west of Beaulieu Road, where further attractions include Bishop's Dyke and areas of exceptional New Forest bog. The dyke was a medieval earthwork constructed in 1284 at the behest of John de Pontoise, Bishop of Winchester, possibly to create an area of marsh that would attract wildfowl. The flora and fauna along the way are truly exceptional, with naturalists being able to spot marsh gentian and bog orchid, damselfly and large marsh grasshopper, redshank and snipe ... as well as the ubiquitous New Forest ponies!

Distance – 3 miles.

OS Outdoor Leisure 22 The New Forest. GR 348064.

A leisurely and easy walk, with the plethora of paths providing the only difficulty.

Starting point The Shatterford car park, just west of Beaulieu Road Station and the pub.

How to get there Beaulieu Road Station lies three miles east of Lyndhurst on the B3056 Beaulieu road. Just to the west of the station, park in the Shatterford car park. Across the railway line from the Shatterford car park lies the Beaulieu Road Inn.

THE PUB

'Whether you simply want to refresh yourself with one of our real ales, or wish to enjoy our excellent restaurant, you can be assured of service in the highest of English tradition at the **Beaulieu Road Inn**.' This is the proud boast of this fine hostelry, whose attractive floral displays inevitably catch the eye of the passing motorist. The extensive menu – from sandwiches and ploughman's through to New Forest venison steak – will include something to cater for every taste. Further details on this hostelry can be found by visiting the web site www.beaulieuroadinn.co.uk

Open 11 am to 3 pm and 6 pm to 11 pm.
☎ 02380 292342

1 Pass through the gate at the southern end of the car park, and follow a track that heads to the south across the open heathland with the railway line on the left-hand side. Continue along this track for ¾ mile, cross two bridges over an area of wetland.

Ahead is a patch of woodland containing a number of silver birch trees. Keep right at a fork, pass these trees and continue to a crosstrack some 50 yards from a gate leading into **Denny Lodge Inclosure**.

2 Turn right on reaching this crosstrack, and follow a prominent path for ¾ mile until, 150 yards before Denny Wood, the path crosses a couple of footbridges over streams. Enter **Denny Wood**, and follow the main path ahead through the woodland until it reaches the road leading to Denny Lodge in 250 yards. Turn right, and follow this driveway for 300 yards to a wooden barrier on the right, at the foot of a gentle hill.

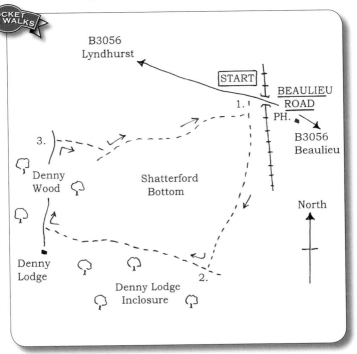

An inquisitive local at Beaulieu Road.

3 Turn right, and follow a grassy ride into a clearing. Keep on the path beyond this clearing which borders the edge of the tree cover before emerging onto **open heath**. Follow the path for 100 yards to a junction, turn left and continue along the prominent track for ½ mile back to the Shatterford car park, the roofs of some cottages at Beaulieu Road acting as a landmark to aim for.

Places of interest nearby

The New Forest Visitor Centre and Museum in Lyndhurst should be the first port of call for any visitor to this fine area of outstanding natural beauty. Audio-visual displays tell the story of the New Forest, its history, traditions, characters and wildlife. The complex also includes the New Forest Embroidery and Gift Shop.

☎ *02380 283444 for further information.*

Beaulieu itself can boast a number of major attractions. As well as the National Motor Museum, there is Beaulieu Abbey and the Palace House, formerly the Great Gatehouse of the abbey. Detailed information on these attractions can be found at www.beaulieu.co.uk

☎ *Telephone: 01590 612345.*

Buckler's Hard is a picturesque 18th century village on the banks of the Beaulieu River. Historically, it is famed as the place where some of the ships of Nelson's fleet were built, a history that can be explored through the 'Buckler's Hard Story' in the Maritime Museum. For more information, visit www.bucklershard.co.uk

☎ *01590 616203.*

13 Keyhaven

The Gun Inn

Keyhaven's small harbour lies on the north Solent shoreline, a quiet and relatively unspoilt corner of what is often a hectic stretch of water. To the north-east of Keyhaven lies an area of marsh, mud flats and creeks. Level tracks, lanes, fieldpaths and a section of the Solent Way are followed across this fascinating landscape, where the vast numbers of sea-birds make field-glasses an absolute necessity! Terns, the grey phalarope, ruff and the little stint are but four of the delightful species found in the pools that lie on the landward side of the coast path, whilst the foreshore is rich in waders, with turnstones, oystercatchers, lapwings and redshanks being just a few names to conjure with. If you simply enjoy a walk with views, then the Solent Way brings a fine outlook across to the Isle of Wight.

THE PUB

The whitewashed **Gun Inn** at Keyhaven has a decidedly nautical feel, with its attractive frontage being adorned with a lifebuoy, ships' lights and a rudder. This should come as little surprise, with this cosy 17th-century hostelry having a location overlooking a boatyard and the sea, with the distant Isle of Wight on the horizon. The Gun offers a good, generous choice of food, often based upon local ingredients, whilst the range of real ales might include Ruddles Best and Old Speckled Hen.

Open 11 am to 3 pm and 7 pm to 11 pm.
☎ *01590 642391.*

Distance – 5 miles.

OS Outdoor Leisure 22 The New Forest. GR 306915

A flat coastal excursion.

Starting point The public car park in Keyhaven.

How to get there Leave the A337 three miles west of Lymington, and take the B3058 into Milford on Sea. From Milford, follow the waymarked – but unclassified – road east into Keyhaven, pass the Gun Inn and park in the public car park on the left (fee payable).

Hampshire

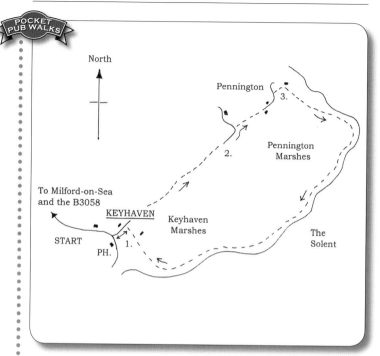

1 Leave the car park, turn right past the Gun Inn and, almost immediately, turn right along a cul-de-sac. In 250 yards, having passed Keyhaven's harbour, continue along the lane until it ends at a gateway. Continue ahead along a gravel track for ¾ mile across **Keyhaven Marshes**. Pass through another gateway and join a lane by a parking area.

2 Follow the lane ahead for 350 yards, pass around a sharp left-hand bend and, in 50 yards, turn right along an enclosed and waymarked footpath. On reaching a lane in 250 yards by **Oxey Farmhouse**, keep ahead along what is a quiet byway past a number of isolated properties. In 175 yards, turn right down the driveway leading to Creek Cottage. Just before the property

itself, pass through a squeeze stile on the right and join the **Solent Way**.

3 Follow this path as it runs along the top of a raised causeway above the creek. Continue along this path around **Oxey Marsh** before bearing in a south-westerly direction back towards Keyhaven, with fine views of the Isle of Wight across the Solent. In 2 miles, the path joins the lane walked at the outset in Keyhaven. Turn left, pass the local harbour on the left and, at the next junction, turn left back to the Gun Inn.

The peaceful Keyhaven Harbour.

Places of interest nearby

Hurst Castle is situated at the seaward end of the shingle spit which extends 1½ miles from Milford-on-Sea. The end of the spit, only ¾ mile from the Isle of Wight, was the perfect location to defend the western approach to the Solent. The castle was built by Henry VIII as one of a chain of coastal fortresses and was completed in 1544. Charles I was imprisoned here in 1648 before being taken to London to his trial and execution. Hurst Castle can be reached by ferry from Keyhaven itself.

☎ *01590 642344 for information on this fascinating attraction.*

St Barbe Museum and Art Gallery in Lymington tells the special story of the coastal strip between the New Forest and the Solent and hosts a changing programme of high-quality exhibitions. The area has seen a thriving salt industry, smugglers landing their illegal cargoes on the coast and a long tradition of innovative boat building. The museum's aim is to capture the unique flavour of life in the district and to bring first class art exhibitions into the town.

☎ *01590 676969 for information or visit the museum's website at www.stbarbe-museum.org.uk*

14 Meonstoke

The Bucks Head Inn

The River Meon, running alongside the Bucks Head in Meonstoke, is the most easterly of the Hampshire chalkstreams. Rising at East Meon and reaching the sea in the Solent 15 miles to the south, the river lent its name to the local railway which ran from Alton to Fareham. The line achieved its place in history in June 1944 when Churchill's war cabinet stayed in a special train in the long siding at Droxford Station – just south of Meonstoke – whilst final preparations for the D-day landings were being made at Southwick House. The trackbed, now a cycle and footpath, returns the walk to Meonstoke after some fine walking on nearby Old Winchester Hill. Owned and managed by English Nature, this is the location

Hampshire

Distance – 6 miles.

OS Explorer 119 The Meon Valley. GR612202.

Steep hillsides – an energetic excursion.

Starting point The Bucks Head Inn at Meonstoke. There is room for careful roadside parking in the vicinity of the inn.

How to get there *Just south of the junction of the A32 with the B3035 in Corhampton, turn into Meonstoke. Having crossed the River Meon, the Bucks Head Inn is on the left.*

of one of Hampshire's finest hill forts, which covers some 140 acres. All around is traditional chalk grassland, where sheep-grazing helps to maintain an area of downland that is home to a rich array of flora and fauna, including several varieties of orchids and numerous butterflies.

THE PUB Situated on the banks of the River Meon, the **Bucks Head** is a charming 17th-century inn that remains very much at the heart of village life. A true country inn, with open fires in the winter and a large river garden, this is a warm and friendly place that also offers superb hospitality. Along with excellent real ales – including Greene King IPA and Ruddles County – there is a menu of traditional English dishes. These might include steak and ale pie and shepherd's pie, and are made using ingredients sourced from local suppliers wherever possible.

Website: www.thebuckshead.com
Open 11 am to 2.30 pm and 7 pm to 11 pm.
☎ *01489 877313*

1 Walk up the road past the Bucks Head to a junction by a small green. Turn left and, almost immediately, follow **Pound Lane** as it bears right. In 300 yards, at a minor crossroads, keep ahead along the main road and continue for 400 yards to a sharp left-hand bend. On this bend, turn right along a track and, at a junction in 100 yards, keep left along the public bridleway. Follow this track for ¾ mile to its junction with a hilltop road, just past the buildings of **Pondside Farm**. Turn left, and continue past some masts to a crossroads in 450 yards.

2 Turn left and, in 250 yards, turn left at a gate and stile to follow a waymarked footpath. Follow the path downhill along the right edges of two fields to reach a lane, and follow the cul-de-sac opposite towards Old Winchester Hill. In 600 yards, having passed **Stocks Cottage** and the adjoining farm buildings, continue along a grassy track to reach a gate at the foot of **Old Winchester Hill**. Beyond this gate, follow a path to the right

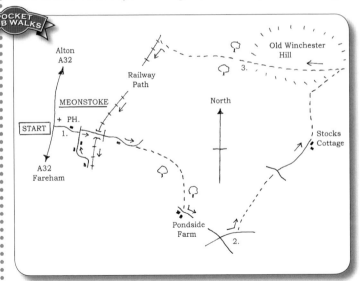

Along the way.

that climbs the hillside to a gate at the top just before some ramparts. Turn right, and follow the path that runs below the ramparts to the eastern end of the hill fort. Turn left, pass through the ramparts and follow the path across the middle of the hilltop enclosure. Having passed through the western end of the hill fort, continue downhill to a gate at the entrance to some woodland.

3 Walk through the woodland and continue along an enclosed path for 200 yards to a junction of paths. Keep ahead on the main enclosed path, and follow what is the **South Downs Way**

for ¾ mile until the right of way bears left into a belt of trees. Follow the track ahead that bears left – and then right – up the embankment onto the **Meon Valley Railway Path**. Follow the trackbed to the left for ½ mile until a path bears left down to a lane. Cross this lane, and follow the path opposite back up onto the trackbed. Continue along the trackbed for ½ mile until, 100 yards before the second bridge that crosses the railway path, there is an exit point on the right. Leave the railway path, and follow the lane downhill for 150 yards, then bear right into the High Street. Walk along this quiet lane for 350 yards to a junction by a small green, before turning left and back to the Bucks Head.

Places of interest nearby

Hinton Ampner, a National Trust propertry a few miles north of Meonstoke, is one of the great gardens of the 20th century. It is a masterpiece of design by Ralph Dutton, 8th and last Lord Sherborne, uniting a formal layout with varied and informal plantings in pastel shades. It boasts a 12-acre garden of year-round interest with scented plants and magnificent vistas over parkland and rolling Hampshire countryside. The house is tenanted but can also be visited and contains a fine collection of English furniture, Italian paintings and hardstones items.
☎ *01962 771305 for further information.*

In Bishops Waltham, a few miles west of Meonstoke, visitors can explore a moated bishop's residence built in 1135. Subsequently destroyed, the residence was then reconstructed as a palace. It was fortified during the Civil War. The buildings that remain date mainly from the 12th and 14th centuries, and include a Great Hall and a three-storey tower.
☎ *01489 892460 for further information.*

The Queen's Head

This walk explores the village of Titchfield, a thriving port and market town in medieval times on account of its abbey. Although a mile or two inland from the Solent, the village was linked to the sea by a navigable channel, thought to be one of the earliest canals in Britain. Away from Titchfield, the coastal path alongside the Solent brings extensive views of the Isle of Wight, as well as the busy sea lanes on the approaches to Southampton. Alongside the Solent is Titchfield Haven National Nature Reserve, a well-known birdwatching site. It covers 369 acres of the Lower Meon Valley and contains a variety of wetland habitats, some of which have become rare in lowland Britain. The reserve is managed primarily for birds but it also has rare flora including rarities such as slender bird's-foot-trefoil, frogbit and marsh mallow. It is also home to foxes, deer, dragonflies and butterflies.

THE PUB

With its handsome black-and-white exterior, the **Queen's Head** stands proudly on the Square in Titchfield. Named after Catherine of Braganza, who married Charles II in Titchfield Abbey, the Queen's Head is proud of its traditional English pub atmosphere. Old local pictures, window seats, dark beams and a central brick fireplace, add to the charm of this historic hostelry. With a menu that features poultry and steak dishes, vegetarian and fish options, as well as an interesting selection of salads, the Queen's Head offers something to delight every taste. There is also a good selection of ever-changing real ales, that might include Greene King or Hop Back.

Open 11 am to 3 pm and 6 pm to 11 pm every day.
☎ *01329 842154*

Distance – 5 miles.

OS Explorer 119 Meon Valley and Portsmouth. GR 540057.

Lanes, tracks and fieldpaths that cross a flat landscape bordering the Solent.

Starting point Church Street in Titchfield.

How to get there Leave the M27 at junction 9, and follow the A27 in the direction of Fareham. Leave the A27 at the second roundabout and follow the unclassified road signposted to Titchfield. In the Square in the centre of the village, turn into Church Street and park on the roadside. The Queen's Head pub is at the far end of the Square, two minutes walk from Church Street.

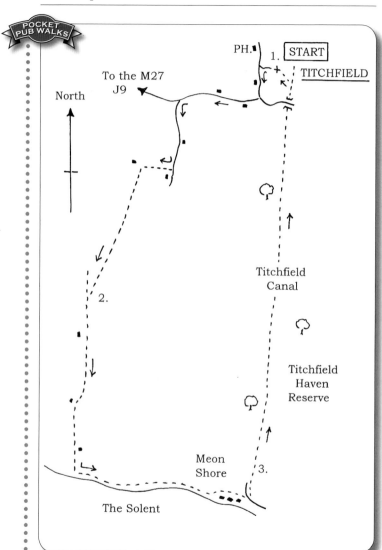

POCKET PUB WALKS

PH.

1. START

TITCHFIELD

To the M27 J9

North

Titchfield Canal

Titchfield Haven Reserve

2.

Meon Shore

3.

The Solent

1 Walk down Church Street to the **Square**, turn left into South Street and continue along to a roundabout by the Coach and Horses pub. Turn right up Coach Hill and, in 350 yards, take the third turning on the left called **Posbrook Lane**. In 600 yards, just before a row of red-brick properties on the right, turn right along an unmetalled lane signposted as a footpath. At a junction in 250 yards, at the end of the field on the left, turn left and follow the path along the whole length of an arable field. At the far side turn right and follow the field boundary to a gap in the far right corner of the field and an unmetalled road.

2 Turn left and follow this road for ¾ mile until, by a barn, it bears right to Lower Brownwich Farm. Turn left through a gateway just past the barn, and follow a track for 350 yards down to the shingle shoreline of the Solent. Turn left, and walk along the coast for ¾ mile to the chalets at **Meon Shore**. The sea-views from the cliff-top path are, in places, obscured by trees and bushes – you may prefer to walk along the foreshore. Pass to the left of the chalets – the beach here is private – and continue along to the lane that comes down to the coast from Titchfield. Cross this road, pass through a wooden barrier and enter **Titchfield Haven Nature Reserve**. Turn left, and follow a path for 250 yards to a point where the path bears left to pass through a squeeze stile to join the towpath alongside the remains of the Titchfield Canal.

3 A brief detour to the left will bring you to the Sea Lock. For the main walk, turn right, and follow the canal – situated in the overgrown ditch on the left – for two miles to a road on the edge of **Titchfield**. Ignore all of the bridges that cross the canal along the way, keeping to the eastern bank of the canal all the while. Cross the road, and continue following the path opposite for 250 yards to a bridge. Cross this bridge, enter the churchyard in Titchfield, and walk around to the front of the church and Church Street.

Hampshire

Titchfield Abbey: Although an impressive ruin, this castellated, fortified manor house bears very little resemblance to the monastery that was founded here in 1232. Notwithstanding its fairly uneventful history, Titchfield Abbey was seen as an important centre, in view of its short distance from

The foreshore at Titchfield Haven.

Winchester, and its close proximity to the sea at that time.

Portsmouth, with its great naval traditions, lies just a few miles from Titchfield. As well as HMS *Victory*, visitors to the city can also explore the remains of the *Mary Rose* as well as HMS *Warrior*, the world's first iron-hulled armoured battleship powered by steam as well as sail and constructed of wrought iron. For visitors interested in the history of the city, there is the Portsmouth City Museum, whilst in Old Commercial Road, the city can also boast the birthplace of Charles Dickens. Neighbouring Southsea is home to a Natural History Museum, as well as Southsea Castle and the D-Day Museum and Overlord Embroidery.

For full details on any of these attractions, contact the city's Tourist Information Centre on ☎ 02392 826722.